Just the Facts

Alzheimer's Disease

Jim McGuigan

Community High School Dist. #94
326 Joliet Street
West Chicago, IL 60185

Heinemann Library
Chicago, Illinois

Customer Service 888-454-2279
Visit our website at www.heinemannlibrary.com

Produced by Monkey Puzzle Media
Designed by Jane Hawkins
Originated by Ambassador Litho Ltd.
Printed and bound in China by South China Printing Company

08 07 06 05 04
10 9 8 7 6 5 4 3 2 1

Library of Congress Cataloging-in-Publication Data
A copy of the cataloging-in-publication data for this title is on file with the Library of Congress.
Alzheimer's disease / Jim Mcguigan
ISBN 1-4034-5143-5

Acknowledgments
The publishers would like to thank the following for permission to reproduce photographs:
Alamy pp. 1 (Sam Tanner/Photofusion), 12 (Plainpicture), 19 (Sam Tanner/Photofusion), 25 (Paul Baldesare/Photofusion); Corbis pp. 14 (DiMaggio/Kalish), 21 (Vo Trung [NPP] Dung/Sygma), 28 (Jose Luis Pelaez, Inc), 35 (Paul Barton), 45 (Michael Heron), 51 (Leland Bobbé); Photofusion pp. 15 (Paul Doyle), 34 (Paul Chitty), 39 (Joanne O'Brien), 41 (Joanne O'Brien); Rex Features pp. 17 (Sipa), 18 (Guzelian Photography); Sally and Richard Greenhill p. 42 (Sally Greenhill); Science Photo Library pp. 4 (Alfred Pasieka), 7 (Simon Fraser/MRC Unit, Newcastle General Hospital), 8 (Antonia Reeve), 9 (Dr W Crum, Dementia Research Group/Tim Beddow), 11 (National Library of Medicine), 20 (SIU), 37 (Chris Priest), 38–39 (Catherine Pouedras), 48 (James King-Holmes), 49; Topham Picturepoint pp. 5 (Image Works), 16 (Bob Daemmrich/ Image Works), 23 (Nita Winter/Image Works), 26 (Alison Wright/Image Works), 31 (Richard Lord/Image Works), 32 (Rhoda Sidney/Image Works), 47 (Jeff Greenberg/Image Works); Wellcome Trust p. 10.

Cover photograph: main image: Science Photo Library/Will and Deni McIntyre; second image: Science Photo Library/ Dr. W. Crum, Dementia Research Group/Tim Beddow.

Every effort has been made to contact copyright holders of any material reproduced in this book.
Any omissions will be rectified in subsequent printings if notice is given to the publisher.

The case studies in this book are based on factual information. In some case studies and elsewhere in this book, names or other personal information may have been changed or omitted in order to protect the privacy of the individuals concerned.

Contents

Alzheimer's Disease 4

What Is Alzheimer's Disease? 6

Other Types of Dementia 8

History of Alzheimer's Disease 10

A Family Connection? 12

Environmental Triggers 14

How Common Is Alzheimer's? 16

A Growing Concern 18

Early Signs and Symptoms 20

Living with Alzheimer's Disease 22

Coping with Memory Loss 30

Care and Support 32

Treatment .36

People to Talk To 42

Professional Care 44

Legal Matters 46

How Can Modern Science Help? 48

Looking to the Future 50

Information and Advice 52

More Books to Read 53

Glossary 54

Index 56

Alzheimer's Disease

Alzheimer's disease is a progressive condition that affects the brain, eventually leading to the death of brain cells. It is referred to as a progressive disease because the condition gradually becomes worse over time. Alzheimer's disease usually strikes people over the age of 65, but it can develop in people as young as 35, when it is called early-onset disease.

This photograph shows two brain scans. The right side is healthy tissue, and the left side shows shrinkage of brain tissue in a person with Alzheimer's disease.

Alzheimer's disease attacks nerve cells in the brain and robs people of their memories. People not only forget the names of everyday objects, they may also forget what these objects are. People with Alzheimer's disease may suddenly find themselves lost even in familiar surroundings.

The on-going damage to the brain eventually leaves Alzheimer's sufferers barely able to speak. Sometimes they are unable to recognize their own husband, wife, or children, and they need help to eat, wash, dress, and to go to the bathroom. This may occur five, ten, or even twenty years after the disease is discovered, although most people enter the final stages of the illness after about eight years.

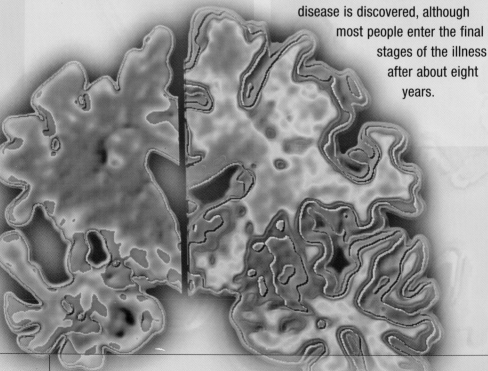

A growing problem

As more people live into their 70s and 80s, Alzheimer's disease affects more lives. By the year 2025, it is estimated that throughout the world there will be more than 34 million people with Alzheimer's disease—incredibly, that is roughly the same amount as the entire population of California.

Expert care

No one can provide proper care for a person with Alzheimer's disease without the support of their family, professionals such as nurses and counselors, and the generous help of people working for voluntary Alzheimer's organizations around the world. Many people, including family doctors, are not familiar with the symptoms of the disease and it may take years for a person to receive a correct diagnosis. Increasing knowledge and awareness of Alzheimer's disease should be the first step on the road to improving the future care of the millions of people who will be lost to this incurable illness.

❝When my mother was diagnosed with Alzheimer's disease I contacted the Alzheimer's Society. They saved my life. The information and advice they gave me helped me and my family get through very difficult times.❞

(Anne Robinson, host of the TV quiz show *The Weakest Link*)

What Is Alzheimer's Disease?

Alzheimer's disease is a form of dementia. The term dementia is used to describe many different diseases of the brain that cause people to experience serious memory loss and confusion. About 1 in 20 people over the age of 65 develop dementia. More than half of these people have Alzheimer's disease, making it the most common cause of dementia. (Other forms of dementia are discussed on pages 8–9.)

A progressive disease

Alzheimer's disease is a progressive condition that affects a person's brain cells. This means that the brain cells gradually die and more parts of the brain become damaged. The person's symptoms will eventually become worse.

People experiencing the early stages of Alzheimer's disease may become forgetful or have difficulty finding the right words for everyday things. One of the first symptoms is the loss of short-term memory (the ability to remember recent events). For example, a 70-year-old person may remember details of their twelfth birthday party, but just a few minutes after leaving the table, they may forget that they have eaten breakfast. As the disease progresses, they may become increasingly confused. Over time the person with Alzheimer's disease will need increasing help in all activities from those who care for them.

A chemical imbalance

People with Alzheimer's disease have a shortage of important chemicals in the brain called neurotransmitters. Neurotransmitters are responsible for the transmission of messages within the brain. These messages control functions such as memory, ability to think clearly, speech, and movement. In Alzheimer's disease, fine fibers of a protein called tau become twisted together to form tangles inside brain cells. These tangles build up until

A scientist examines brain tissue of a person with Alzheimer's disease under a microscope. The dark areas shown on the screen consist of thick layers (plaques) of the protein beta amyloid.

they burst the cells, causing them to die. Another protein, beta amyloid, builds up in layers called plaques in between the brain cells. These plaques are toxic (poisonous) to the brain cells and kill any cells close to them.

As different parts of the brain become damaged, the person with Alzheimer's disease gradually loses abilities— although each person will experience the disease in their own individual way. Usually, the part of the brain that is responsible for storing new memories is affected first. Later the part of the brain that is responsible for planning and carrying out tasks becomes damaged. In the final stage of the disease, the area of the brain that controls the muscles is affected, making walking and other movements difficult.

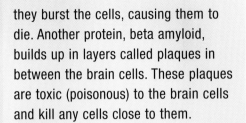

Other Types of Dementia

It is important for doctors to be able to tell the difference between Alzheimer's disease and other types of dementia. A correct diagnosis will allow the person to get the best treatment and know what to expect from their illness. The various dementias have similar symptoms to Alzheimer's disease, but are not the same thing.

Vascular dementia

Vascular dementia is caused by too little blood reaching the brain. The person usually suffers a small stroke.

This involves the death of a small group of brain cells that are starved of blood for a minute or two. The small blood vessels, which normally carry blood to the brain cells, may be blocked for a short time by blood clots or they may have burst as a result of high blood pressure. One small stroke is often followed by another, and several of these mini strokes can damage the brain, making the person forgetful and confused.

Vascular dementia can occur when high blood pressure causes a blood vessel going to the brain to burst. People who tend to have high blood pressure need to have it checked regularly.

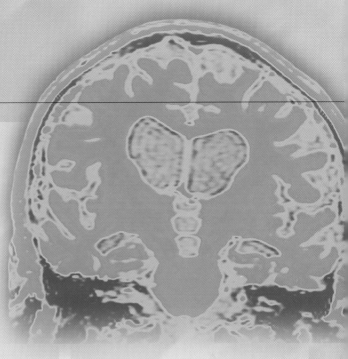

Dementia with Lewy bodies

In this kind of dementia, tiny round blobs of protein called Lewy bodies build up in brain cells. They disrupt the normal functioning of the brain, leading to memory loss, an inability to think clearly, and difficulty with speaking or writing.

Frontal lobe dementia and Pick's disease

Most damage in frontal lobe dementia and Pick's disease occurs in the front part of the brain. This part of the brain is responsible for personality, behavior, and language skills. People with these forms of dementia may suddenly start to swear more or behave inappropriately. They may also find it difficult to make plans.

Alcohol-related dementia

People who drink too much alcohol over a long period of time may cause damage to the part of the brain that controls short-term memory. People with this condition may also have difficulty acquiring new information or skills.

This scan shows a section of the brain of a person who has dementia with Lewy bodies. The brain (shown in red) has atrophied (shrunk), leaving holes (shown in blue) at the bottom left and right, and large, fluid-filled areas in the center.

Creutzfeldt-Jacob disease (CJD)

Creutzfeldt-Jacob disease (CJD) results from prions (infectious protein particles) attacking the nervous system and the brain, causing dementia. CJD progresses rapidly and is often fatal within one year. In 1994 a special form of CJD, called Variant CJD, was identified. It affected people of all ages and is believed to have been caused by eating meat from cows suffering from a similar disease called bovine spongiform encephalopathy (BSE)—also known as mad cow disease.

History of Alzheimer's Disease

Symptoms of memory loss and confusion, similar to those of Alzheimer's disease, have been described in ancient Egyptian, Greek, and Roman texts. Descriptions of dementia-like illnesses have also been recorded throughout the centuries. But it was not until the early 20th century that Alzheimer's disease was recognized as a condition in its own right.

Middle Ages

In Europe in the Middle Ages, many scholars thought that all mental illnesses, including what we now call Alzheimer's disease, were caused by evil spirits entering a person and taking control of their body and mind. Treatments could be very harsh, and many people were chained up and beaten in an attempt to drive away the evil spirits.

Asylums

In the 18th century a more rigorous form of scientific and medical thinking began to spread throughout the world. It became known as the Age of Enlightenment. People were now less interested in following traditional beliefs and wanted to gain greater knowledge and understanding (enlightenment) by using logic and reason. People with dementia were often sent to asylums (institutions that were specially built to hold mentally ill people). Asylums were unpleasant places, over-crowded with people who were often chained up and mistreated.

It was not until the mid-1850s that an increased understanding of mental illness brought significant changes in the whole approach to treatment.

This hospital in Paris, in 1857, was one of the first for patients with mental illnesses, including dementia.

Most people were then taken out of asylums and cared for in hospitals. Doctors began actively studying mental illnesses in an attempt to find out what caused them.

Recent discoveries

In 1906 a German neurologist, Dr. Alois Alzheimer, found peculiar changes in the brain tissue of a woman who had died from what was thought to be an unusual mental illness. The woman, named Auguste, suffered from depression, hallucinations, and dementia and died at only 55 years old. Experts soon realized the importance of the discovery and named the condition Alzheimer's disease. Alzheimer's disease was thought to be a rare illness until the 1970s, when experts realized that most people who had senile (old age) dementia and pre-senile (young age) dementia actually had Alzheimer's disease.

The first drug treatments for Alzheimer's disease were developed during the 1990s. These treatments were unable to cure the disease but could at least slow down the progression of symptoms for a little while.

Dr. Alois Alzheimer, who first identified the disease.

A Family Connection?

Alzheimer's disease does sometimes run in families. But this is very rare, and explains only part of the picture. In most cases the disease seems to strike people randomly. More research is needed to explain why.

Genes and early-onset disease

Some people develop Alzheimer's disease between the ages of 35 and 65. This is called early-onset disease. Although rare, about 50 percent of

people with early-onset disease have inherited the condition from their parents through a defective (faulty) gene.

Genes are like tiny pieces of information that determine everything about us, from our eye or hair color to the way our bodies grow and develop, including our likelihood of developing certain medical disorders. Genes are arranged inside 23 pairs of chromosomes (threadlike structures that are found in every cell in the body). There are millions of different ways that the genes can be arranged on the 46 chromosomes. This makes it difficult to determine which genes might be defective.

One clue came when scientists noticed that almost all people born with Down's syndrome develop the tangles and plaques in the brain associated with Alzheimer's disease (see pages 6–7). Due to a genetic error, people with Down's syndrome have a third copy of chromosome 21. Experts studied this chromosome and found a defective gene, which allows a build-up of an abnormal protein, beta amyloid, in the brain. This stops brain cells from working properly (see page 7). Only a small number of people who have the inherited form of early-onset disease have this defective gene.

Other defective genes have been found on chromosomes 1 and 14. If someone with one of these defective genes has children, half of those children will go on to develop Alzheimer's disease in later life. For the average person, however, the chance of developing early-onset disease is only 1 in 1,000.

Late-onset disease

No one is sure what causes late-onset disease. Once a person is over the age of 65, the risk of developing Alzheimer's disease increases to about 1 in 30. Some scientists believe that genes may play a part in the development of this condition. On their own, however, it seems unlikely that genes cause late-onset disease. This suggests that the genes only make a person more likely to get the disease. There needs to be something in the environment, such as a toxic substance in their diet, to actually trigger the disease.

Environmental Triggers

While defective genes may make it more likely for a person to develop Alzheimer's disease later in life, people with these genes do not necessarily go on to have the disease. Scientists believe that a combination of various environmental factors may trigger the condition. A number of theories have been put forward, some of which are listed below.

Auto-immune disease

Auto-immune diseases are disorders in which the body's immune system, which normally fights foreign invaders such as bacteria and viruses, starts to attack some of its own cells. Some scientists think that in some older people, changes in the aging brain cells may cause the immune system to attack the brain, resulting in Alzheimer's disease. An infection or chemical in the diet may trigger this possible pathway to the disease.

Prion/slow virus theory

Tiny infectious protein particles called prions have been identified as a cause of some brain disorders that are similar to Alzheimer's disease. Some experts suggest that prions or slow viruses (viruses that cause disease many years later) may be a trigger for Alzheimer's disease.

Head injuries

Alzheimer's disease is unusually common in people who have had whiplash injuries to their neck and head. It is not clear how this injury might cause the disease, and it may just be a coincidence that it is more common in people who have had whiplash injuries. However, the finding that boxers, too, suffer more often than other people from dementia suggests that neck and head injuries may trigger the disease.

Boxers have a high risk of suffering head and neck injuries.

Aluminum and mercury

Some small research studies have suggested that aluminum might be directly involved in the development of Alzheimer's disease. However, most experts now believe that this is very unlikely.

Another theory suggested that the mercury used years ago for filling cavities in teeth might have leaked out and somehow caused Alzheimer's disease. This is now thought to be unlikely, but more research is being done.

Reducing the risk

Increasing evidence suggests that what is good for the heart is also good for the brain. Keeping fit and healthy may reduce the risk of developing all forms of dementia. General advice includes:
- Not smoking
- Eating a healthy diet (a diet low in salt and fat, and high in fresh fruit and vegetables), which can help reduce blood pressure
- Exercising regularly
- Getting your blood pressure checked regularly
- Avoiding head injuries (for example, wearing a helmet for cycling).

How Common Is Alzheimer's Disease?

Alzheimer's disease is very rare in young people but becomes more and more common as people age. Up to the age of 65, only 1 person in 1,000 will develop the disease. But in people over the age of 85, it affects one person out of every three.

It can happen to anyone

Anyone can get Alzheimer's disease. Since announcing to the world he had Alzheimer's disease in 1992, former U.S. president Ronald Reagan and his wife, Nancy, have raised millions of dollars for research into Alzheimer's disease. Other famous people with Alzheimer's disease have helped raise awareness of the condition.

The life of British novelist Dame Iris Murdoch, who died in 1999 after a long struggle with Alzheimer's disease, was the subject of the film *Iris*.

Funding research

The research funds and extra publicity attracted through the work of famous people is very helpful. But the governments of every nation in the world have to provide better funding for research into all forms of dementia and for better care for the millions of people affected by it. In the United

Every little step counts: Sponsored walks such as this one in Austin, Texas, raise much-needed money for research into Alzheimer's disease.

States, about four million people suffer from dementia. In the United Kingdom, an estimated three quarters of a million people have dementia— more than 18,000 of them are under the age of 65. Almost two-thirds of these people have Alzheimer's disease.

It is estimated that 66 percent of all the people in the world with Alzheimer's disease live in developing countries. Yet these countries often lack doctors, nurses, occupational therapists and counselors to help people with the disease and to support those who care for them.

Famous people with Alzheimer's disease

- Rita Hayworth (1918–1987), U.S. film star of over 40 films, including *Only Angels Have Wings* and *Gilda*.
- Charlton Heston (1924–), U.S. film star of such epic movies as *Ben-Hur* and *The Ten Commandments*.
- Iris Murdoch (1919–1999), British novelist and philosopher. Her best-known books include *The Bell* (1958) and *The Sea, the Sea* (1978).
- Ronald Reagan (1911–), former actor and U.S. president (right).

A Growing Concern

Over the next 25 years the number of people with Alzheimer's disease and other forms of dementia is expected to increase dramatically. More people are living past the age of 65, and the chances of developing Alzheimer's disease get higher as people grow older. In addition, there was a boom in the number of babies born after World War II. In 25 years, many of these people will be reaching their 70s and 80s and developing Alzheimer's disease.

It is difficult to determine exactly how many people throughout the world have Alzheimer's disease because not all countries recognize the disease or keep count of how many people develop it. Not everyone will have been specifically diagnosed with Alzheimer's disease. Some countries only keep count of people with all types of dementia, but we know that more than half of them will have Alzheimer's disease.

Estimating figures

Experts estimate that there are 18 million people with dementia in the world today, 9 million of whom have Alzheimer's disease.

By the year 2025, there will be about 34 million people with dementia. By 2050 it is estimated that this number will grow to 70 million. By this time, about 70 percent of people with dementia will live in developing countries, such as Brazil and India. In the United States, where the elderly population is growing rapidly, it is predicted that the number of people with dementia will grow from 4 million now to 16 million by the year 2050.

Counting the cost

This rising tide of people with dementia will have a huge impact on the many people directly caring for them. Many will have to give up their jobs to care for their loved ones 24 hours a day. U.S. experts have estimated that it will cost 61 billion dollars a year—enough to buy 600 trans-Atlantic airliners—to treat and care for all the people in the United States with dementia. Much of this cost will be to cover the lost wages of people who might have to give up their jobs to care for someone with the disease.

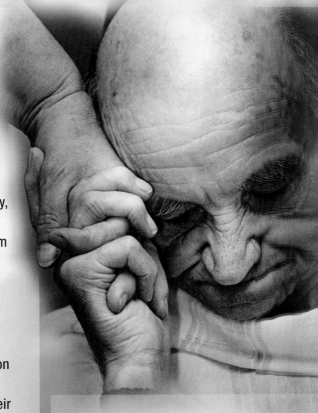

❝There is an urgent need for more research into the causes, prevention, and treatment of this devastating disease.❞

(Stephen McConnell, president and chief executive officer of the Alzheimer's Association, United States, July 2002)

Early Signs and Symptoms

It can be difficult to spot the first symptoms of different types of dementia. When a grandparent becomes more forgetful, it may just seem to be part of getting older. But when the family looks more closely, it may become clear that the person is behaving much differently than normal.

People in the early stages of Alzheimer's disease may seem more absent minded, misplacing things or repeating themselves. They may sometimes be confused and do odd things such as putting the milk in the oven instead of the fridge. However, it is often only when a person has been diagnosed with Alzheimer's disease that close friends and family can look back and realize that the small changes in behavior were probably the beginning of the condition.

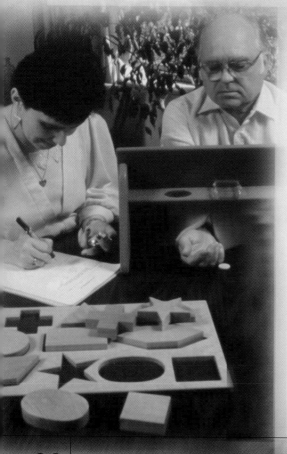

Memory tests

To help make a diagnosis, a doctor may use a simple memory test. This might include asking a few basic questions about recent events and past memories, such as:
- How old are you?
- What is your date of birth?
- What is the day today?
- What month are we in?
- What year is it?
- When was World War I?
- What is the name of the president?
- Where are you now?
- Remember an address, such as 20 Elm Street, and repeat it after five minutes.
- Count backwards from 20 to 1.

This man is taking part in a timed memory test to see if he can remember shapes correctly.

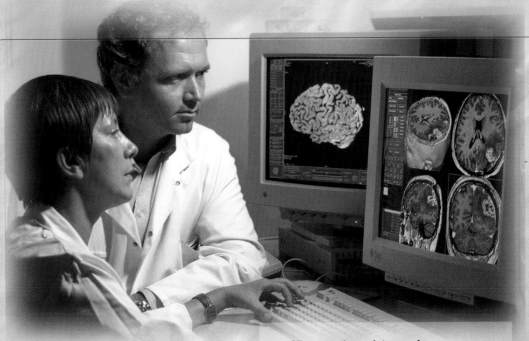

CT scans show pictures of cross sections through the brain.

Making a diagnosis

No single test can show for certain that a person has Alzheimer's disease. But doctors may use brain scans, memory tests, and blood tests to rule out other illnesses. This enables them to make a correct diagnosis roughly 90 percent of the time.

A brain scan may provide a picture of the changes taking place in a person's brain. Brain scans can be done in several different ways, including a special type of X-ray technique called computerized tomography (a CT scan) to show pictures of slices through the brain. Another type of scan is called a magnetic resonance imaging scan (MRI scan). The MRI scan produces a more detailed image of the brain using radio signals produced by the body in response to the effects of a very strong magnet inside the scanner.

❝I'd check my toothbrush for wetness to see if I'd brushed my teeth, I'd check my towel to see if I'd had my shower.❞

(Marilyn Truscott, a Canadian scientist who was diagnosed with Alzheimer's disease in 1998)

Living with Alzheimer's Disease

Everyone who has Alzheimer's disease will experience it in their own way. Generally speaking, the condition can be looked at as a series of stages in which the symptoms gradually become worse over time. However, many of these symptoms may appear earlier or later, or not at all.

Progression of Alzheimer's

Alzheimer's disease usually begins with small changes in a person's behavior or abilities. A common sign is short-term memory loss (other early signs are mentioned on page 20). It is important for caregivers not to do things for the person that they can manage to do themselves; patients will feel better if they continue to remain independent for as long as they can. Certain memory skills people learned when they were much younger, such as playing a musical instrument, or swimming the breaststroke, may survive for many years into the illness. This may be because these involve a different type of memory called procedural memory—a "how to do things" form of memory that appears to escape damage longer than other memory systems.

During the middle stage, a person with Alzheimer's disease will need more and more support to help them with everyday tasks, such as cooking, eating, washing, and going to the bathroom. Their memory loss will worsen, and names may become more difficult to remember. Other symptoms include failing to recognize family members, or confusing one person with another. Some people at this stage get more upset or angrier than they used to. They may become restless and suffer insomnia (an inability to sleep). Some people get confused about where they are, or wander off and become lost.

During this stage the person with Alzheimer's disease may put themselves or other people at risk of harm through their forgetfulness. For example, they may turn on a gas stove and forget to light it, allowing gas to leak out, which could cause an explosion. Damage to the part of the brain responsible for behavior may cause them to behave inappropriately, such as going outside for a walk in their pajamas. Some people may even have hallucinations (seeing or hearing something that is not really there).

Some people with Alzheimer's disease will need help to get dressed.

"My memory might not be as good as it was, but it doesn't stop me from being me."

(Anonymous person with Alzheimer's disease, quoted in the book *Tangles and Starbursts* by Sharon Bailey and Julia Darling)

Advanced stages

People with Alzheimer's disease may eventually need constant care throughout the day and night. They may lose their memory completely and not be able to recognize family members. They may become very weak and have difficulty walking since the part of the brain that controls movements of the muscles becomes damaged by the disease. It is important to remove things—such as loose rugs, electrical cords, or shoes and other clutter lying on the floor—that might increase their risk of falling.

Some people with Alzheimer's become so frail that they have to stay in bed or use a wheelchair. Eating can become very difficult, since they have trouble swallowing food properly, and they are likely to become thinner—though a few eat more and put on weight. At this stage, they may become incontinent, which means they lose control of their bladder, and they may also lose control of their bowels. Many people remain at home and are cared for by their family throughout the course of their illness.

Others eventually go into a nursing home, where nurses and other professional people provide very good full-time care for them. This is often not possible in developing countries where there are few nursing homes.

Once the disease has progressed this far, people tend to talk very little due to the increased damage to the parts of the brain responsible for speech. Sometimes they become restless and seem to be looking for someone or something. They may suddenly become aggressive or very upset, especially if they feel threatened in some way.

Love and reassurance

But although the person may not even recognize close family members and not seem to understand what anyone says to them, they are still able to respond to kindness and gentleness. It can be reassuring if their hand is held and someone talks to them in a calm soothing voice. Or they may enjoy smelling flowers or scented candles or listening to music.

People with Alzheimer's disease may become frail during the advanced stages and may find it difficult to walk.

"My mother's need for love continued until the end. In her last days, as she lay there, she still responded to a gentle massage, soothing music, or soft voices."

(Jayne, from Alaska, who cared for her mother who had Alzheimer's disease)

DJ's story

Nineteen-year-old DJ Rodie, a student at McGill University in Montreal, Canada, was eight years old when his grandmother, Addie, first began to show symptoms of Alzheimer's disease. Before she was ill, he remembers the great fun they had, talking and joking, when they went to feed the geese in the park. "She would do anything to make me laugh—even chase a few geese."

Addie started to have trouble handling everyday tasks, such as driving over to pick up DJ from his music lessons, or going to the supermarket and remembering which foods she needed. She also began to find it hard to do simple math, which was very surprising because she had worked as an accountant and had been very good at arithmetic. Addie began to lose things and get confused. She would search through every room in her house looking for her sister—even though her sister lived many miles away and had not come to visit. It was then, at the age of 71, that Addie was diagnosed with Alzheimer's disease.

DJ's parents soon realized that Addie could no longer live on her own, and they helped her move in with them. After moving in she kept saying she wanted to go home to her mother and father. DJ's mother and father tried to explain to her that her own parents had died. But each day she forgot and she felt the sadness of losing them again. Sometimes the best way though the difficult times was to make jokes. DJ's dad would say if Addie's parents were still alive then they owed him 50 years worth of birthday presents!

As the disease developed, Addie could no longer talk to DJ or remember the words of the songs they used to sing together. Addie has now moved into a nursing home where DJ frequently visits her. He says "I'm no longer able to have deep conversations with my grandma, but I can definitely still give her a hug—I can still tell her that I love her very much."

> **"I know there will come a day when she will no longer be able to recognize me, but I believe she'll still be the same loving, caring person that I spent countless hours with."**
>
> **(DJ Rodie of Montreal, Canada, whose grandmother has Alzheimer's)**

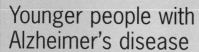

Younger people with Alzheimer's disease

Although Alzheimer's disease is much more common in people over the age of 65 than in younger people, it does affect many people in their 40s and 50s. In the United States there are 60,000 people under the age of 65 with dementia, and about 18,000 in the United Kingdom. Many doctors often do not realize that people this young can develop dementia and do not even consider Alzheimer's disease in their diagnosis. It can take years of tests and examinations before the disease is correctly diagnosed.

When someone develops Alzheimer's in their 40s or 50s, the family faces especially difficult challenges.

Sometimes it is a relief for the person with Alzheimer's disease to know what is wrong with them. Later, it is the family that worries more, seeing the person they love change as their illness progresses. The family may also have the pressure of money worries since the person with Alzheimer's disease and their main caregiver are no longer able to work.

Young families affected by Alzheimer's disease face many challenges. It can be difficult for children and young adults to face the fact that, just when they feel they need their mother or father most, he or she cannot support them, and instead needs their help.

❝I cannot run away from it. I cannot hide under a stone ... it's there and I've got to deal with it.❞

(Mary, 43, from New Zealand, whose husband has Alzheimer's disease)

Mary's story

Mary Reid, from Tauranga, New Zealand, has been caring for her husband, Michael, since he developed Alzheimer's disease. Their three children, Alicia (15), Brendan (13), and Christopher (10), have also been helping to care for Michael, who was only 44 when he was diagnosed. Michael, who worked as a butcher, had been asked to take a week off work because he was acting strangely. At home he was also doing odd things, such as getting up for work at midnight and taking a shower, when he did not need to be up until after 5 a.m. "One night," Christopher remembers, "Dad was standing by the pantry and I asked him if I could have a drink. He said, 'Where's the pantry?' and he was standing right beside it – that was pretty scary."

Mary says that the organization Alzheimer's New Zealand has been a great support, talking through problems and encouraging Michael to take part in group activities.

Michael's illness progressed rapidly, and he is now living in a nursing home, where his family visits him regularly.

Coping with Memory Loss

One of the biggest problems for people with Alzheimer's disease is losing their short-term memory. They may not remember that they had breakfast, and start to have it all over again. This kind of memory loss can give the person an unsettling sense of losing control. Caregivers can do a lot to help during the early stages of the illness. It is important for caregivers to listen to the patient's fears and frustrations, offer reassurance, and consider practical ways that might help.

Memory joggers

Some people with early stage Alzheimer's disease find memory joggers, such as to-do lists, diaries, and clear, written instructions useful. Not being able to remember loved ones' names is often upsetting. A big display board with photos of family and friends with names clearly marked may help.

Keeping to a routine

It is helpful to stick fairly closely to a routine in which daily activities take place at about the same time each day. This makes the person feel less anxious since it is easier for them to remember what usually happens during the day. It also helps if certain food items or other everyday objects are always put back in the same place.

"I remember an ex-Royal Air Force pilot who had Alzheimer's and used to come to our support meetings. He used to sit there hardly saying a word. Then one day we had a slide-show on military aircraft, and up he was, chatting away to the presenter."

(Barrie Randall, team leader of an Alzheimer's Society voluntary support group in Reading, United Kingdom)

Memories from the past

One of the first parts of the brain that becomes damaged by Alzheimer's disease is the part that is responsible for forming new memories. However, memories from the distant past remain clear until much later in the course of the illness. It is important to make every effort to share these early memories with the person. While the person is in the early stages of their illness it can be helpful to start a scrapbook of their life. This should spark quite a few memories from long ago. The scrapbook will also help anyone else who steps in later to care for the person to know more about who they are.

Looking through a photo album together may spark distant memories, untouched by Alzheimer's disease.

Care and Support

Because of the progressive nature of the condition, caring for someone with Alzheimer's disease can eventually become a full-time job. It might not be quite so difficult at the start of the illness, but as the disease progresses, activities such as going to the bathroom, washing, dressing, eating, and sleeping become more and more difficult for the person with Alzheimer's disease. It is important to allow the person to do what they can for as long as possible. This may mean allowing them to spend much more time getting dressed, for example.

In the early stages of the illness, a caregiver can often help the person with Alzheimer's disease to stay active.

Everyday activities may be a little easier to manage when things are always put back in the same place.

Caregivers should try to get to meetings at their local Alzheimer's support group to share experiences with other people dealing with the illness. Physical skills, such as riding a bike or playing golf, are not lost as quickly as memory skills, so these pastimes should continue for as long as the person with Alzheimer's disease is able to enjoy them.

Challenging behavior

Caregivers need to deal tactfully and respectfully with any situation where the person with Alzheimer's disease refuses to take part in a particular activity, such as taking a bath or changing into clean clothes. Some people with Alzheimer's disease may simply not remember why they need to wash, and they may not recognize when their clothes are dirty. Keeping a routine such as always running the bath just before bedtime can sometimes make things easier.

A person with Alzheimer's disease may behave inappropriately, such as getting undressed at the dinner table. It is important for caregivers to remember that they have simply become confused about where they are and what time it is.

Being safety conscious

All family members need to help the person with Alzheimer's disease to reduce any risks to their personal safety. For example, they could make sure the person does not have access to matches or lighters.

"We had taken my Nan out to a posh restaurant. Just as we began to eat our meal, she opened her purse, pulled out a pair of underwear and threw them on the table. We all laughed loudly, including my Nan."

(Sarah, from Berkshire, United Kingdom. She helped care for her grandmother, who died at age 71 of Alzheimer's disease.)

A difficult time

Caring for a mother, father, or grandparent with Alzheimer's disease can be very demanding. Many caregivers must cope with a wide range of feelings. They may feel angry, sad, tired, depressed, fed up, guilty, or scared. It is perfectly normal for someone to have any or all of these feelings at different times. It can be easier for people to cope if they can talk about their feelings with other members of the family, a good friend, or a healthcare professional such as a counselor.

Support for caregivers

Caregivers are likely to get sick themselves if they try to do everything on their own. They need to seek help from other members of the family, and from professionals such as social workers. Social workers can help find someone to care for the person with Alzheimer's disease during the day to give the caregiver an opportunity to rest.

Social workers may arrange for meals to be delivered to the person's home, to give the main caregiver a break.

A young caregiver may find that they fall behind with their homework or are too tired to concentrate at school. The school needs to be told what is happening at home. Teachers can then help, perhaps by finding extra time for the young caregiver to talk to a tutor, or by finding them a quiet place to do their homework at lunchtime. It is vital that caregivers take the time to eat properly, exercise (such as swimming or walking), and maintain other relationships (such as going to the movies with friends).

Young caregivers may feel tired or depressed. It usually helps if they find someone to talk to.

Michael's story

Michael, thirteen, from Gisborne, New Zealand, found it very difficult when his grandfather and grandmother, who both had Alzheimer's disease, came to live with him and his parents.

When his grandfather died, Michael's grandmother seemed to take it out on him. "She got really angry with me, throwing cups of tea at me and telling me to get out of her house," he says. "That really upset me. I always try to be respectful and nice to Gran. She doesn't really know what she's saying or doing. When Mom goes out, I give Gran her tea. At first she used to refuse to eat it because I gave it to her, but now she's OK about it. Sometimes at night after Mom's put her to bed she gets up, so I go and get her back to bed."

Treatment

No drugs can cure Alzheimer's disease, but some can slow down the speed at which people's symptoms get worse. These drugs are cholinesterase inhibitors. They stop an important chemical called acetylcholine from being removed from the brain. Acetylcholine is a neurotransmitter that helps brain cells pass messages to one another. Studies have shown that people with Alzheimer's disease do not have enough acetylcholine.

Everyone is different

Cholinesterase inhibitors are not suitable for everyone with Alzheimer's disease. They tend to be prescribed only for early to middle stages of the disease. Medical experts in each country have to agree on rules to determine which people should take these inhibitors. It may be, for example, that someone's disease has gone so far that the drugs would do them no good. Every person reacts to the drugs in a slightly different way. Some people have a noticeable improvement, while others are not helped at all. But if someone is helped, the beneficial effects usually last for about one year.

Before prescribing drugs, doctors have to think about the possible side effects. The side effects include dizziness, headaches, nausea, vomiting, and diarrhea. Many people will cope with these unwanted side effects, but for others they may be so upsetting that they cancel out any benefits of the drugs. Different people may have different side effects, and they do not last for the same length of time for everyone.

A new treatment?

A new type of drug called memantine may be the first drug that can temporarily stop Alzheimer's disease from damaging the brain. It is the first drug that can be taken by people with middle- or late-stage Alzheimer's disease. Scientists need to do more extensive studies to confirm the results found in a small number of people who were given memantine.

A doctor has to assess how the illness is affecting an individual before deciding which medicine may help.

After taking the drug, people seem to think a little more clearly and behave more normally. Memantine appears to protect healthy brain cells from being killed by excess amounts of a neurotransmitter called glutamate that leaks out of cells that have been damaged by Alzheimer's disease. Each person responds differently. Some improve, some remain stable, and in other people it has no effect. Side effects include hallucinations, dizziness, and headaches.

Alternative treatments

There are many non-drug treatments, also called alternative therapies, that may help with Alzheimer's disease. These approaches cannot cure the illness, but they may relieve some of the symptoms or improve the quality of life for the person with Alzheimer's disease and their family. Alternative therapies should never be used to replace the medicines prescribed by the person's doctor, but they may be useful to take in addition to the usual medicine. The person or their caregiver should check with their doctor before trying any alternative therapy, as it may react badly with other medicines they are taking. Some alternative therapies are listed here.

Acupuncture

In this ancient Chinese therapy, very fine needles are pushed into the skin to help with healing. It seems that acupuncture could have some benefit in Alzheimer's disease, but more studies are needed.

Herbal remedies

The herbal remedy *Ginkgo biloba*, which comes from the Chinese Ginkgo tree, appears to reverse some of the memory difficulties of Alzheimer's disease. Many studies are being carried out with this herbal treatment, which causes very few unwanted side effects.

Aromatherapy

Aromatherapy is the use of pleasant-smelling oils and plant extracts to help relax a person or encourage a feeling of comfort. In Alzheimer's disease, aromatherapy may also have more specific benefits. Research has shown that aromatherapy using the scent of the lemon balm plant may help prevent the loss of the neurotransmitter acetylcholine—one of the key chemicals that allows brain cells to communicate with each other.

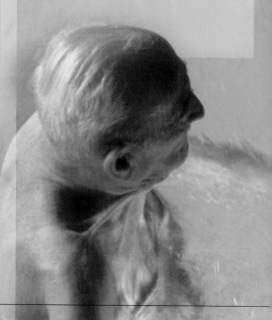

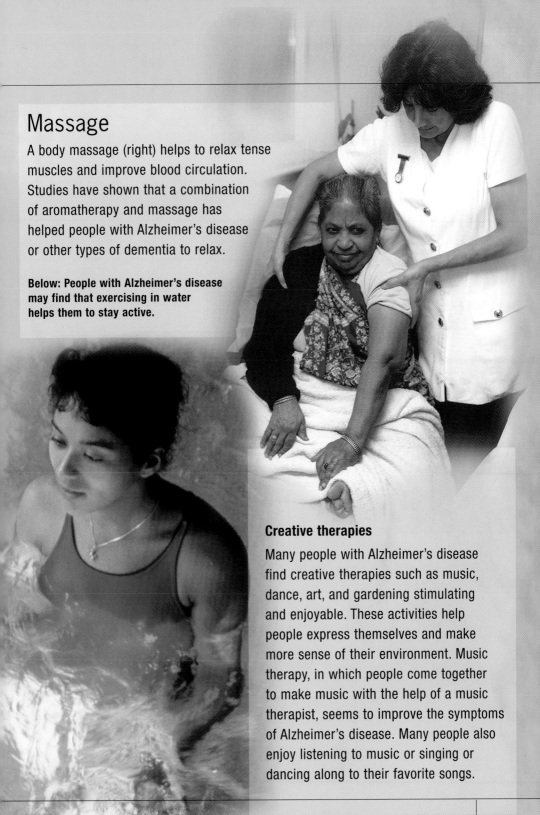

Massage

A body massage (right) helps to relax tense muscles and improve blood circulation. Studies have shown that a combination of aromatherapy and massage has helped people with Alzheimer's disease or other types of dementia to relax.

Below: People with Alzheimer's disease may find that exercising in water helps them to stay active.

Creative therapies

Many people with Alzheimer's disease find creative therapies such as music, dance, art, and gardening stimulating and enjoyable. These activities help people express themselves and make more sense of their environment. Music therapy, in which people come together to make music with the help of a music therapist, seems to improve the symptoms of Alzheimer's disease. Many people also enjoy listening to music or singing or dancing along to their favorite songs.

Reminiscence therapy

Psychological therapies, such as reminiscence therapy, can be helpful to some patients with Alzheimer's disease. In reminiscence therapy, the person is shown photographs or videos, perhaps of cars, airplanes, or movie stars from their youth. This often brings back many memories. Copies of old advertisements for breakfast cereals, canned goods, and other foods can be used to make modern cereal boxes and canned foods look like they did when the person was at school or in their first job. Some caregivers have borrowed dresses, suits, and other clothes that were fashionable when the person was young to help encourage memories of enjoyable nights out for patients at dances and parties.

Therapists usually provide reminiscence therapy to small groups of people with Alzheimer's disease. By sharing their memories with the group, they can feel proud about their achievements, make new friends, and feel less lonely. Reminiscence therapy can be good for caregivers, too, as they get to know more about their loved one, and learn things from them that helps to increase their respect for the person and understand them more. The aim of this therapy is to emphasize what they can remember rather than what they have forgotten.

Many local branches of Alzheimer's support groups throughout the world have collections of photos, videotapes, and other objects that may be helpful for reminiscence therapy.

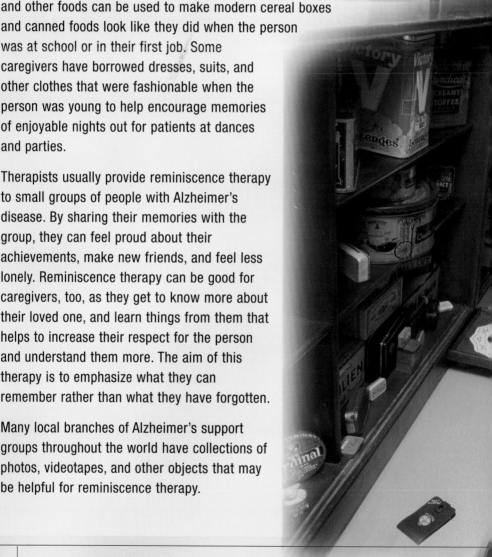

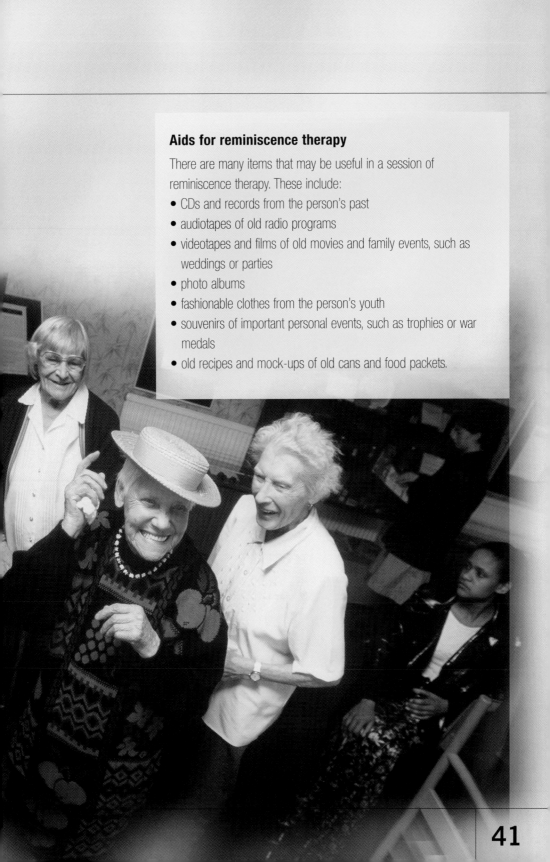

Aids for reminiscence therapy

There are many items that may be useful in a session of reminiscence therapy. These include:

- CDs and records from the person's past
- audiotapes of old radio programs
- videotapes and films of old movies and family events, such as weddings or parties
- photo albums
- fashionable clothes from the person's youth
- souvenirs of important personal events, such as trophies or war medals
- old recipes and mock-ups of old cans and food packets.

People to Talk To

Alzheimer's disease affects the whole family. So it is important for everyone to talk to one another, share feelings, and be supportive. But sometimes help is needed from healthcare professionals with special skills and training, whose job involves working with families affected by Alzheimer's disease. These include social workers, community nurses, counselors, and family doctors.

Voluntary organizations such as the United States Alzheimer's Association and United Kingdom Alzheimer's Society provide booklets and brochures about Alzheimer's disease. For people who want to find out more, local groups hold regular meetings for people with Alzheimer's disease and for caregivers so they can share experiences and offer each other support.

❝When someone feels that they have a better understanding of the illness and are not so fearful, then I feel I have made some difference.❞

(Anne Deck, Alzheimer's counselor)

Helplines

Many organizations operate telephone lines to provide information and support regarding any aspect of Alzheimer's disease. (See pages 52–53 for further details.) Many organizations have local groups run by volunteers. These offer advice and assistance, and usually hold regular meetings during which people with Alzheimer's disease and their caregivers can meet, share experiences, and offer each other support.

Listening to others with similar problems and sharing experiences with people that understand can be very uplifting.

Alzheimer's associations around the world provide practical and emotional help and information to families affected by the disease. They also put pressure on governments to spend more money on services to help care for people with Alzheimer's disease.

Religious leaders

If the person with Alzheimer's or their caregiver has religious faith, they may find it helpful or comforting to talk to a priest, minister, rabbi, or other spiritual leader. It may be helpful and calming for the person to continue to attend religious services. If this is no longer possible, it may be possible for caregivers to make arrangements for their spiritual leader to visit them at home.

Help on the web

Most national Alzheimer's support organizations have websites that offer the latest research news and information about the disease. Many have a message board where people with Alzheimer's disease can communicate with others around the world. Caregivers can also share their experiences with other caregivers. The websites give addresses and telephone numbers for all local voluntary support groups and services.

Professional Care

While some people with Alzheimer's disease will be cared for at home throughout their illness, others will eventually move into a nursing home. The need for 24-hour care every day can become too much for their family to cope with.

A difficult decision

Moving a mother or father or any other loved one out of their own home into a nursing home is a difficult thing for any family to do. Sons and daughters may feel that they have let the person down, or worry that the person will not get the same loving care they got at home. By finding out about all the available options, and visiting a number of different homes, the family can choose the best possible care for their relative.

Different types of home

The main difference between a residential home and a nursing home is that the nursing home has trained nurses who can provide nursing care for people with Alzheimer's disease at any time of the day or night. Both types of home will help the person with dressing, washing, and going to the bathroom, and will give them meals and take them on walks.

Choosing a home

It is important to find the right kind of nursing home for the person with Alzheimer's disease. It has to be in a place that is easy for family and friends to visit, and that feels friendly and welcoming. The family will want

to find a place where people are gently encouraged to take part in activities, such as exercising to music, singing, or talking.

Many caregivers look for a home in which there is enough room for everyone to sit together during the day if they want to, and which has a safe garden for people to sit in or go for walks in.

By talking to other people living in a nursing home, the family can find one that will suit their loved one. Some people will want a place where they have their own bedroom; they might also like to have their favorite chair or other furniture. The nursing home manager can let the family know if furniture and other personal things can be brought into the home. Regular visits by the family will help the person settle into a good nursing home.

Legal Matters

It is important that the person with Alzheimer's disease and their family sort out important legal matters while the person is still able to do so. For example, they will need to prepare for a time in their illness when they will no longer be able to pay their own bills and manage their money. The person may also wish to consider what forms of treatment they would or would not like to have later in their illness, when they may be too confused to understand the options available to them.

Power of attorney

A power of attorney document is a legal form with which one person gives one or more people the power to manage their money and property. The person with Alzheimer's disease (or other forms of dementia) can choose for this to happen while they are mentally capable of understanding what they are doing, or they may choose for power of attorney to come into effect only when they are mentally incapable.

The process of setting up a power of attorney document is complicated and usually requires the help of a legal expert. Because this is a legal document, it must be set up while the person is aware of what is involved and can show that they understand the process. For this reason, it must be done while the symptoms of the disease are still mild.

It is important for a person with Alzheimer's disease to seek legal advice before the illness progresses.

Living wills

A living will is a legal document that allows people to state what forms of treatment they would or would not like to have in the future. A living will only concerns a person's medical treatment and has nothing to do with an ordinary will, which states what is to happen to a person's money and property after their death. The person's doctor will keep a copy of the will with their medical records to ensure their instructions are followed. An example of the kind of instruction the person may make in their living will might be that they are to be given no special medical procedure or treatment aimed at prolonging their life.

Different countries have different laws regarding living wills, and changes continue to be made. In the United Kingdom, Canada, and many states in the United States, living wills are legally binding: Doctors have to follow their instructions or risk breaking the law.

How Can Modern Science Help?

New drugs that promise to slow down the progression of Alzheimer's disease and to lessen memory loss and other symptoms are currently being researched. But no cure for the disease looks likely to be discovered in the near future. The Human Genome Project, an international study to identify every single gene in the human body, will help in the understanding of how faulty genes cause Alzheimer's disease. It may then be possible using gene therapy techniques to repair these genes and prevent Alzheimer's disease from developing. However, this research is still at an early stage and it will be many years before we know how effective gene therapy may be.

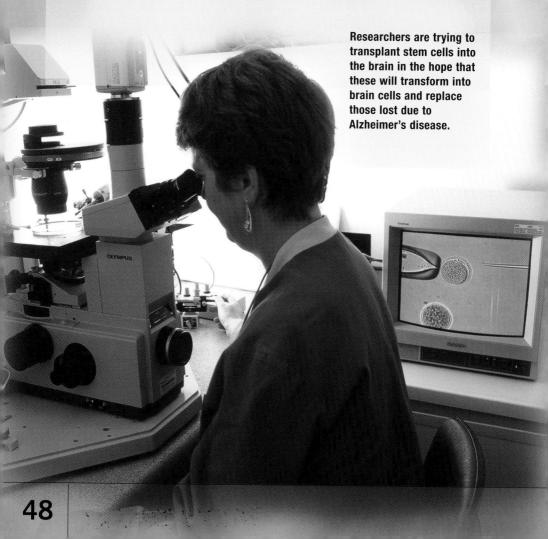

Researchers are trying to transplant stem cells into the brain in the hope that these will transform into brain cells and replace those lost due to Alzheimer's disease.

Stem cell transplants

Another possible area of research involves stem cells. These are special cells, found in bone marrow and other organs, that can develop into a wide range of different types of cells, such as liver or stomach cells. In studies with mice, research has shown that stem cells from bone marrow transplanted into the heart, for example, will change into heart muscle cells. Scientists are now studying the possibility that stem cells transplanted into the brain of a person with Alzheimer's disease may develop into brain cells that might replace those lost due to the disease.

Vitamin therapy

Another area of research deals with giving people extra vitamin E and C. It is thought that these may be able to help protect the brain from some of the damage caused by Alzheimer's disease.

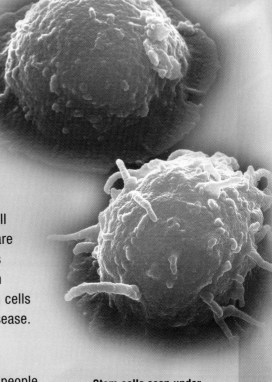

Stem cells seen under a powerful microscope.

Stem cell research

Scientists in Melbourne, Australia recently discovered that the brain contains stem cells. Experts had always thought that once nerve cells died they could not be replaced. But the discovery of stem cells suggests that dead nerve cells can be replaced. Why then can the brain not heal itself when damaged by diseases like Alzheimer's? It could be that it is unable to grow new nerve cells fast enough to repair the damage. Scientists are developing new drugs that could increase the rate at which stem cells can transform into nerve cells. This could lead to big improvements in the quality of life of people with Alzheimer's disease.

Looking to the Future

People are living longer than ever before, and older people are becoming a larger proportion of the population. As the population of older people grows, so does the number of people affected by Alzheimer's disease. Many people throughout the world are now full-time caregivers for people with the disease.

Training for caregivers

As well as dealing with the effects of the condition, people with Alzheimer's disease and their families often have expensive bills to pay for medical tests, treatments, and nursing home costs. Caregivers should be given information about the disease and training to help them care for someone with the disease. A study from Australia has shown that people who receive such training and information do a better job and suffer less stress.

Raising public awareness

The world community needs to ensure that it takes into account the needs of people with Alzheimer's disease and their families, and to help them to live as fulfilling a life as possible. More activities in schools are needed to help young people understand the disease.

Improving funding and information

The particular problems posed by Alzheimer's disease in the developing world must not be forgotten. It is estimated that, by 2050, 70 percent of all people with Alzheimer's disease will live in developing countries. These countries will need financial help and knowledge from wealthier countries to ease the enormous suffering the disease will cause. The challenge facing every nation now is to ensure they are ready to help the growing number of people affected by Alzheimer's disease.

> **Everybody whose life is affected by [dementia] will find it easier to be courageous [...] when they know the people around them and their government recognize its appalling nature.**
>
> (Dr. Nori Graham, chairman of Alzheimer's Disease International, speaking at the launch of Alzheimer's World Health Day, in April 2001)

Understanding dementia

In 2002 a successful project called Dementia on Stage targeted fifteen- to seventeen-year-old school students in Western Australia. They were given information about dementia and asked to write pieces of drama for a performance on the stage. A series of sketches called *Alzheimer's Anonymous* was one of the award-winning pieces of drama. Understanding of the issues of dementia greatly increased among students after this project.

Information and Advice

The following organizations, websites, and books can provide a wide range of useful information about Alzheimer's disease and sources of practical support for families affected by this illness.

Contacts

The Alzheimer's Association
Helpline: 800-272-3900
Tel: 1-312-335-8700
Fax: 1-312-335.1110
Website: www.alz.org
This is the largest national voluntary organization and the top private funder of research into the causes, treatment and prevention of Alzheimer's disease. A wide range of information is available on the website, which has a message board, poetry corner and gallery of artwork.

Alzheimer's Disease Education and Referral Center
Website: www.alzheimers.org/
Provides detailed information about Alzheimer's disease and the latest research.

Alzheimer's Disease International
Website: www.alz.co.uk
This organization is an umbrella group of 64 Alzheimer associations throughout the world. It provides information and funds research, including programmes to improve the care of people with Alzheimer's disease in developing countries.

More Books to Read

Willet, Edward. *Alzheimer's Disease.* Berkeley Heights, NJ.: Enslow Publishers, 2002.

Friedlander, Mark P. Outbreak: *Disease Detectives at Work.* Minneapolis, MN.: Lerner Publishing, 2002.

Gosselin, Kim. *Allie Learns about Alzheimer's Disease: A Family Story about Love, Patience, and Acceptance.* Plainview, NY.: JayJo Books, 2001.

Tubbs, Janet. *Alzheimer's Disease.* Scottsdale, AZ: Arcadia Press, 2000.

Glossary

Age of Enlightenment
period in the 18th century when leading thinkers encouraged people to use their own logic to understand the world rather than follow traditional beliefs

alternative therapies
various treatments that people may find helpful in addition to the traditional medical treatments used by doctors

asylum
place where mentally ill people were kept. Although they were meant to be places of shelter and support, they were often overcrowded and made a person's illness worse.

auto-immune disease
disease in which a person's body mistakenly attacks its own cells

beta amyloid
abnormal protein found in clumps throughout the brain in Alzheimer's disease. It is thought to block normal communication between nerve cells.

cholinesterase inhibitors
dementia drugs that stop the breakdown of acetylcholine, the chemical that transmits messages between brain nerve cells

chromosome
thread-like structure inside cells that carries the genes

Creutzfeldt-Jacob disease (CJD)
rare form of dementia caused by an infectious agent called a prion

CT (computerized tomography) scan
X-ray scan that results in a series of pictures of slices through the brain or other organs

dementia
incurable loss of brain function, involving memory, thinking, and concentration. It is caused by injury or brain disease, such as Alzheimer's disease.

depression
mental disorder characterized by feeling extremely gloomy and inadequate and being unable to concentrate. It is quite different from feeling a little down or having the blues.

Down's syndrome
genetic condition in which the person affected is born with an extra chromosome and has various physical problems and a learning disability

early-onset disease
Alzheimer's disease that develops in people younger than 65

frontal lobes
parts of the brain lying just behind the forehead, which are responsible for planning, behavior, and personality

gene
information within body cells that determines a person's characteristics, such as hair color or height. Genes are passed down to us by our parents.

gene therapy
technique in which normal genes are inserted into cells in place of missing or faulty genes to correct genetic disorders

hallucinations
imagined visions or sounds

immune system
body's natural defense against disease and infection

incontinent
unable to control the bladder or the bowels

insomnia
unable to sleep

living will
written statement explaining how a person should be treated medically when they are no longer able to make such decisions themselves

MRI (magnetic resonance imaging) scan
type of scan that produces pictures of body organs using a powerful magnet

neurologist
scientist who specializes in disorders of the brain and nervous system

neurotransmitters
chemicals that act as messengers between the nerve cells of the brain

occupational therapist
person who can advise on ways to help someone maintain their living skills and care for themselves

Pick's disease
rare form of dementia that affects language skills, personality, and memory

plaques
layers of an abnormal form of the protein beta-amyloid, which form in areas between brain cells

power of attorney document
legal document with which one person gives one or more people the power to manage their money and property

prion
infectious protein particle.

protein
compound containing nitrogen, which is an essential part of body tissues such as muscle

reminiscence therapy
treatment that attempts to stimulate people's memories by showing objects they would have seen in their past

short-term memory
type of memory we use to remember recent events

slow virus
virus that causes disease many years after infection

social worker
professional who can offer advice on various social matters

stem cell
cell that can become virtually any type of cell in the body

tangles
in Alzheimer's disease, these are groups of twisted fine fibers of an abnormal form of a protein called tau, which builds up inside brain cells and causes them to burst and die

tau
protein that is essential to support the structure of cells and to transport materials from one part of the cell to another

Index

A acetylcholine 36, 38, 54
acupuncture 38
aging 14
alcohol-related dementia 9
alternative therapies 38–39, 54
aluminum 15
Alzheimer, Dr. Alois 11
aromatherapy 38–39
asylums 10, 54
auto-immune disease 14, 54

B bacteria 14
beta amyloid 6–7, 13, 54–55
boxers 14
brain scan 21
BSE 9

C cholinesterase inhibitors 36, 54
chromosomes 13, 54
confusion 6, 10
creative therapies 39
Creutzfeldt-Jacob disease (CJD) 9, 54–55
CT scan 21, 54

D dementia 8–9, 54
alternative therapies 39
Alzheimer's disease 6
expected increase 18
research 16
symptoms 20
depression 11, 54
diagnosis 5, 8, 20–21
diet 13, 15
Down's syndrome 13, 54
drug treatments 11
new 48

E early-onset disease 4, 12, 28–29, 54
Egyptians 10
environmental triggers 13–15
evil spirits 10
exercise 15

F frontal lobe dementia 9

G gene therapy 48, 54
genes 13–14, 54
Ginkgo biloba 38
glutamate 37
Greeks 10

H hallucinations 11, 23, 37
head injuries 14–15
herbal remedies 38
high blood pressure 8
Human Genome Project 48

I immune system 14, 55

incontinence 24, 55
insomnia 22, 55

L late-onset disease 13
lemon balm 38
Lewy bodies 9
living wills 47, 55

M massage 25, 39
memantine 37
memory loss 4, 7, 30–31
complete 24
dementia 6, 9
history 10
memory tests 20–21
mercury 15
Middle Ages 10
MRI scan 21, 55
Murdoch, Dame Iris 16–17
music therapy 39

N neurotransmitters 6, 36–38, 55

O occupational therapists 17, 55

P Pick's disease 9, 55
plaques 6–7, 13, 55
presenile dementia 11
prions 9, 14, 54–55
procedural memory 22
psychological therapies 40

R Reagan, Ronald and Nancy 16
reminiscence therapy 40–41, 55
Romans 10

S senile dementia 11
short-term memory 55
loss 6, 9, 22
slow virus 14, 55
smoking 15
stem cells 48–49, 55
stroke 8
symptoms 20–21, 27
diagnosis 5
worsening 6, 22

T tangles 6, 13, 55
tau 6, 55

V Variant CJD 9
vascular dementia 8
viruses 14, 55
vitamins 49

W whiplash injuries 14